Published by Angelis Publications
ISBN: 978-1-912484-17-1
www.angelispublications.com

benvinguda
Velkomin
roimh
grata
Croeso
vitajte
üdvözöljük
Bem
vítejte
welkom
menyambut
widziane
Sveiki
benvenuti
Bienvenue
Benvido
maligayang
benvenuti
willkommen
bienvenida
venit
willkommen
välkomna
пожаловать
tervetuloa
mile
Сардэчна
mừng
velkommen
welcome
просимо
dobrodošli
akeyi
Ласкаво
chào
sveikt
Добро
fáilte
vindo

A Welcome Message To Our Guests

Date / Name / From	Comments

Would you be willing to let us share your testimonial? If so, please scribble your initials after your comments. Thank you!

Date / Name / From	Comments

Would you be willing to let us share your testimonial? If so, please scribble your initials after your comments. Thank you!

Date / Name / From	Comments

Would you be willing to let us share your testimonial? If so, please scribble your initials after your comments. Thank you!

Date / Name / From	Comments

Would you be willing to let us share your testimonial? If so, please scribble your initials after your comments. Thank you!

Date / Name / From	Comments

Would you be willing to let us share your testimonial? If so, please scribble your initials after your comments. Thank you!

Date / Name / From	Comments

Would you be willing to let us share your testimonial? If so, please scribble your initials after your comments. Thank you!

Date / Name / From	Comments

Would you be willing to let us share your testimonial? If so, please scribble your initials after your comments. Thank you!

Date / Name / From	Comments

Would you be willing to let us share your testimonial? If so, please scribble your initials after your comments. Thank you!

Date / Name / From	Comments

Would you be willing to let us share your testimonial? If so, please scribble your initials after your comments. Thank you!

Date / Name / From	Comments

Would you be willing to let us share your testimonial? If so, please scribble your initials after your comments. Thank you!

Date / Name / From	Comments

Would you be willing to let us share your testimonial? If so, please scribble your initials after your comments. Thank you!

Date / Name / From	Comments

Would you be willing to let us share your testimonial? If so, please scribble your initials after your comments. Thank you!

Date / Name / From	Comments

Would you be willing to let us share your testimonial? If so, please scribble your initials after your comments. Thank you!

Date / Name / From	Comments

Would you be willing to let us share your testimonial? If so, please scribble your initials after your comments. Thank you!

Date / Name / From	Comments

Would you be willing to let us share your testimonial? If so, please scribble your initials after your comments. Thank you!

Date / Name / From	Comments

Would you be willing to let us share your testimonial? If so, please scribble your initials after your comments. Thank you!

Date / Name / From	Comments

Would you be willing to let us share your testimonial? If so, please scribble your initials after your comments. Thank you!

Date / Name / From	Comments

Would you be willing to let us share your testimonial? If so, please scribble your initials after your comments. Thank you!

Date / Name / From	Comments

Would you be willing to let us share your testimonial? If so, please scribble your initials after your comments. Thank you!

Date / Name / From	Comments

Would you be willing to let us share your testimonial? If so, please scribble your initials after your comments. Thank you!

Date / Name / From	Comments

Would you be willing to let us share your testimonial? If so, please scribble your initials after your comments. Thank you!

Date / Name / From	Comments

Would you be willing to let us share your testimonial? If so, please scribble your initials after your comments. Thank you!

Date / Name / From	Comments

Would you be willing to let us share your testimonial? If so, please scribble your initials after your comments. Thank you!

Date / Name / From	Comments

Would you be willing to let us share your testimonial? If so, please scribble your initials after your comments. Thank you!

Date / Name / From	Comments

Would you be willing to let us share your testimonial? If so, please scribble your initials after your comments. Thank you!

Date / Name / From	Comments

Would you be willing to let us share your testimonial? If so, please scribble your initials after your comments. Thank you!

Date / Name / From	Comments

Would you be willing to let us share your testimonial? If so, please scribble your initials after your comments. Thank you!

Date / Name / From	Comments

Would you be willing to let us share your testimonial? If so, please scribble your initials after your comments. Thank you!

Date / Name / From	Comments

Would you be willing to let us share your testimonial? If so, please scribble your initials after your comments. Thank you!

Date / Name / From	Comments

Would you be willing to let us share your testimonial? If so, please scribble your initials after your comments. Thank you!

Date / Name / From	Comments

Would you be willing to let us share your testimonial? If so, please scribble your initials after your comments. Thank you!

Date / Name / From	Comments

Would you be willing to let us share your testimonial? If so, please scribble your initials after your comments. Thank you!

Date / Name / From	Comments

Would you be willing to let us share your testimonial? If so, please scribble your initials after your comments. Thank you!

Date / Name / From	Comments

Would you be willing to let us share your testimonial? If so, please scribble your initials after your comments. Thank you!

Date / Name / From	Comments

Would you be willing to let us share your testimonial? If so, please scribble your initials after your comments. Thank you!

Date / Name / From	Comments

Would you be willing to let us share your testimonial? If so, please scribble your initials after your comments. Thank you!

Date / Name / From	Comments

Would you be willing to let us share your testimonial? If so, please scribble your initials after your comments. Thank you!

Date / Name / From	Comments

Would you be willing to let us share your testimonial? If so, please scribble your initials after your comments. Thank you!

Date / Name / From	Comments

Would you be willing to let us share your testimonial? If so, please scribble your initials after your comments. Thank you!

Date / Name / From	Comments

Would you be willing to let us share your testimonial? If so, please scribble your initials after your comments. Thank you!

Date / Name / From	Comments

Would you be willing to let us share your testimonial? If so, please scribble your initials after your comments. Thank you!

Date / Name / From	Comments

Would you be willing to let us share your testimonial? If so, please scribble your initials after your comments. Thank you!

Date / Name / From	Comments

Would you be willing to let us share your testimonial? If so, please scribble your initials after your comments. Thank you!

Date / Name / From	Comments

Would you be willing to let us share your testimonial? If so, please scribble your initials after your comments. Thank you!

Date / Name / From	Comments

Would you be willing to let us share your testimonial? If so, please scribble your initials after your comments. Thank you!

Date / Name / From	Comments

Would you be willing to let us share your testimonial? If so, please scribble your initials after your comments. Thank you!

Date / Name / From	Comments

Would you be willing to let us share your testimonial? If so, please scribble your initials after your comments. Thank you!

Date / Name / From	Comments

Would you be willing to let us share your testimonial? If so, please scribble your initials after your comments. Thank you!

Date / Name / From	Comments

Would you be willing to let us share your testimonial? If so, please scribble your initials after your comments. Thank you!

Date / Name / From	Comments

Would you be willing to let us share your testimonial? If so, please scribble your initials after your comments. Thank you!

Date / Name / From	Comments

Would you be willing to let us share your testimonial? If so, please scribble your initials after your comments. Thank you!

Date / Name / From	Comments

Would you be willing to let us share your testimonial? If so, please scribble your initials after your comments. Thank you!

Date / Name / From	Comments

Would you be willing to let us share your testimonial? If so, please scribble your initials after your comments. Thank you!

Date / Name / From	Comments

Would you be willing to let us share your testimonial? If so, please scribble your initials after your comments. Thank you!

Date / Name / From	Comments

Would you be willing to let us share your testimonial? If so, please scribble your initials after your comments. Thank you!

Date / Name / From	Comments

Would you be willing to let us share your testimonial? If so, please scribble your initials after your comments. Thank you!

Date / Name / From	Comments

Would you be willing to let us share your testimonial? If so, please scribble your initials after your comments. Thank you!

Date / Name / From	Comments

Would you be willing to let us share your testimonial? If so, please scribble your initials after your comments. Thank you!

Date / Name / From	Comments

Would you be willing to let us share your testimonial? If so, please scribble your initials after your comments. Thank you!

Date / Name / From	Comments

Would you be willing to let us share your testimonial? If so, please scribble your initials after your comments. Thank you!

Date / Name / From	Comments

Would you be willing to let us share your testimonial? If so, please scribble your initials after your comments. Thank you!

Date / Name / From	Comments

Would you be willing to let us share your testimonial? If so, please scribble your initials after your comments. Thank you!

Date / Name / From	Comments

Would you be willing to let us share your testimonial? If so, please scribble your initials after your comments. Thank you!

Date / Name / From	Comments

Would you be willing to let us share your testimonial? If so, please scribble your initials after your comments. Thank you!

Date / Name / From	Comments

Would you be willing to let us share your testimonial? If so, please scribble your initials after your comments. Thank you!

Date / Name / From	Comments

Would you be willing to let us share your testimonial? If so, please scribble your initials after your comments. Thank you!

Date / Name / From	Comments

Would you be willing to let us share your testimonial? If so, please scribble your initials after your comments. Thank you!

Date / Name / From	Comments

Would you be willing to let us share your testimonial? If so, please scribble your initials after your comments. Thank you!

Date / Name / From	Comments

Would you be willing to let us share your testimonial? If so, please scribble your initials after your comments. Thank you!

Date / Name / From	Comments

Would you be willing to let us share your testimonial? If so, please scribble your initials after your comments. Thank you!

Date / Name / From	Comments

Would you be willing to let us share your testimonial? If so, please scribble your initials after your comments. Thank you!

Date / Name / From	Comments

Would you be willing to let us share your testimonial? If so, please scribble your initials after your comments. Thank you!

Date / Name / From	Comments

Would you be willing to let us share your testimonial? If so, please scribble your initials after your comments. Thank you!

Date / Name / From	Comments

Would you be willing to let us share your testimonial? If so, please scribble your initials after your comments. Thank you!

Date / Name / From	Comments

Would you be willing to let us share your testimonial? If so, please scribble your initials after your comments. Thank you!

Date / Name / From	Comments

Would you be willing to let us share your testimonial? If so, please scribble your initials after your comments. Thank you!

Date / Name / From	Comments

Would you be willing to let us share your testimonial? If so, please scribble your initials after your comments. Thank you!

Date / Name / From	Comments

Would you be willing to let us share your testimonial? If so, please scribble your initials after your comments. Thank you!

Date / Name / From	Comments

Would you be willing to let us share your testimonial? If so, please scribble your initials after your comments. Thank you!

Date / Name / From	Comments

Would you be willing to let us share your testimonial? If so, please scribble your initials after your comments. Thank you!

Date / Name / From	Comments

Would you be willing to let us share your testimonial? If so, please scribble your initials after your comments. Thank you!

Date / Name / From	Comments

Would you be willing to let us share your testimonial? If so, please scribble your initials after your comments. Thank you!

Date / Name / From	Comments

Would you be willing to let us share your testimonial? If so, please scribble your initials after your comments. Thank you!

Date / Name / From	Comments

Would you be willing to let us share your testimonial? If so, please scribble your initials after your comments. Thank you!

Date / Name / From	Comments

Would you be willing to let us share your testimonial? If so, please scribble your initials after your comments. Thank you!

Date / Name / From	Comments

Would you be willing to let us share your testimonial? If so, please scribble your initials after your comments. Thank you!

Date / Name / From	Comments

Would you be willing to let us share your testimonial? If so, please scribble your initials after your comments. Thank you!

Date / Name / From	Comments

Would you be willing to let us share your testimonial? If so, please scribble your initials after your comments. Thank you!

Date / Name / From	Comments

Would you be willing to let us share your testimonial? If so, please scribble your initials after your comments. Thank you!

Date / Name / From	Comments

Would you be willing to let us share your testimonial? If so, please scribble your initials after your comments. Thank you!

Date / Name / From	Comments

Would you be willing to let us share your testimonial? If so, please scribble your initials after your comments. Thank you!

Date / Name / From	Comments

Would you be willing to let us share your testimonial? If so, please scribble your initials after your comments. Thank you!

Date / Name / From	Comments

Would you be willing to let us share your testimonial? If so, please scribble your initials after your comments. Thank you!

Date / Name / From	Comments

Would you be willing to let us share your testimonial? If so, please scribble your initials after your comments. Thank you!

Date / Name / From	Comments

Would you be willing to let us share your testimonial? If so, please scribble your initials after your comments. Thank you!

Date / Name / From	Comments

Would you be willing to let us share your testimonial? If so, please scribble your initials after your comments. Thank you!

www.ingramcontent.com/pod-product-compliance
Lightning Source LLC
Chambersburg PA
CBHW081126300726
48982CB00005B/866

* 9 7 8 1 9 1 2 4 8 4 1 7 1 *